Bird Talk

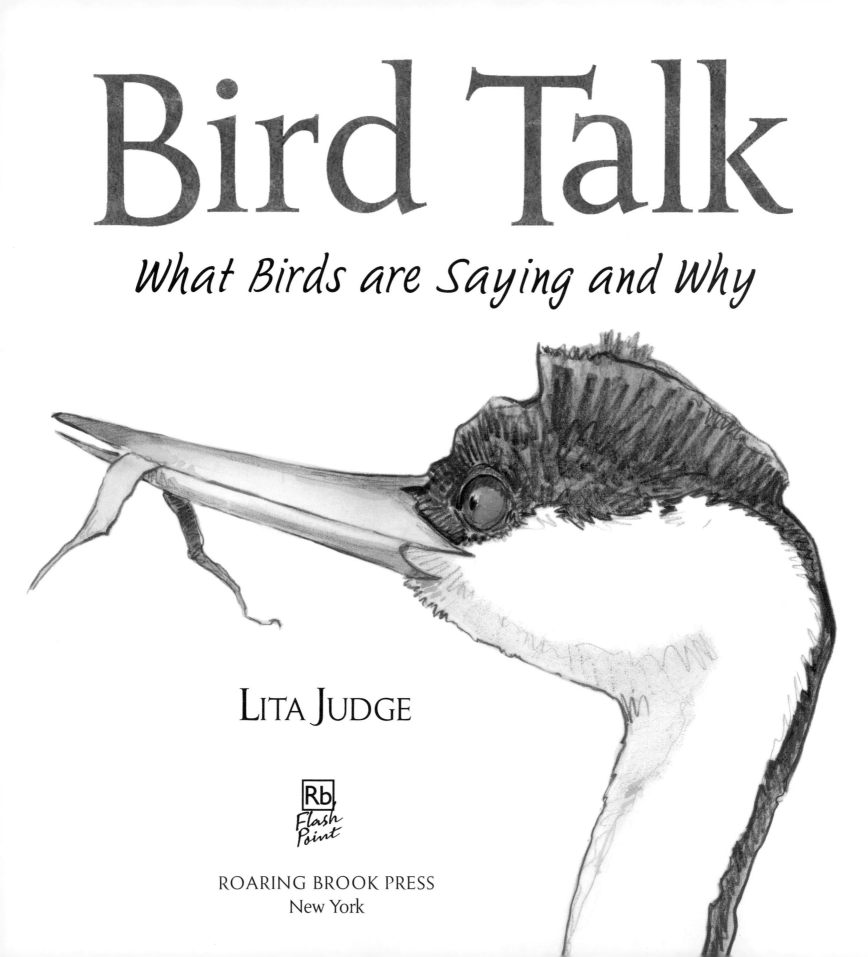

Bird Talk

What Birds are Saying and Why

LITA JUDGE

Rb
Flash
Point

ROARING BROOK PRESS
New York

Chirp, warble, quack,
coo, rattle, screech!

In backyards, meadows, and forests, the air is filled with bird talk.

But what are they saying?

Pick Me!

Male songbirds go all out to
get noticed in the spring.

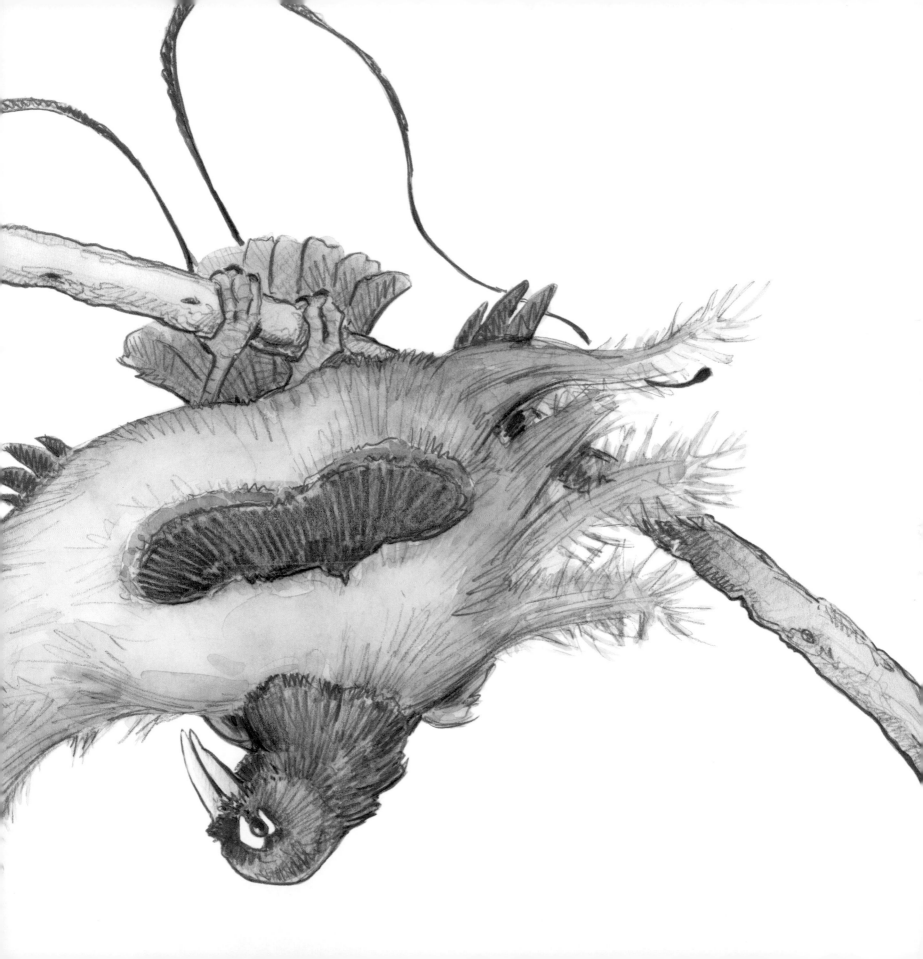

Wahr . . . wahr . . . wahr . . .
A **Blue Bird of Paradise** sings to attract a mate and defend his territory. To make sure a female notices, he flips upside down and swings frantically to and fro.

The melodious song and bright-colored feathers of an **American Goldfinch** say, "Choose me, I'm the healthiest." Like most songbirds, the female is quieter and drabber, the better to sit unnoticed on her nest.

An **American Robin** sings hundreds of different songs. The more complicated his song, the more he says, "I have the most experience. I'll make the best mate."

I'm the strongest.

Not all birds sing to attract mates and claim their territory.
Some males strut,

bang,

and BOOM!

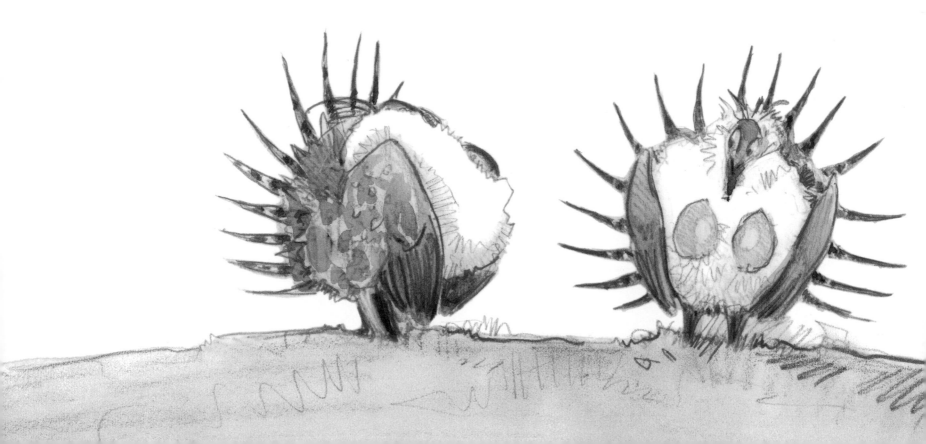

To catch the eye of a female, male **Sage Grouse** puff up their feathers and strut like runway models. Then they make loud popping sounds by blowing up air sacs and rubbing their wings across the chest, *PLOP, plop, kaploop.*

Gobble, gobble, gobble. **Wild Turkeys** strut as well. But their naked heads are covered in wattles that turn scarlet red. The bird with the biggest, brightest wattles usually wins.

A **Palm Cockatoo** is a regular one-man hard-rock band. He whistles and bobs his head. Then he breaks off a stick to drum against a tree. The message is clear to other males, "Stay away! This is MY tree."

Let's do the Blue-Footed Booby dance.

Many birds dance to communicate with a future mate.

Blue-Footed Boobies

don't want to be confused with Red-Footed Boobies. So the male lifts his feet, proudly showing their bright blue color. If a female likes what she sees, she joins the dance, announcing, "We belong together."

Western Grebes dance in perfect unison by running across the water like a pair of water-skiers. After their fancy footwork, the partners present weeds to each other, as if to say, "And this is how we will build our nest."

Indian Sarus Cranes bow and leap, performing an elegant ballet. They trumpet loudly and throw sticks into the air proclaiming, "We are paired. We will build a nest together." Their bond is so strong, they mate for life.

Greetings.

Birds who share nesting duties
have a lot to say to each other.

A pair of **European White Storks** greet one another each time one parent returns to the nest. They throw their heads forward and back, clattering their bills.

A male Rhinoceros Hornbill says, "I will provide" as he brings food to his mate. The female has sealed herself inside a tree nest for three months, incubating eggs and caring for her young.

When a **Northern Gannet** returns from fishing, she and her mate stand on tiptoe over the nest. The one to leave its bill pointing skyward the longest says, "My turn to take off."

Parents and chicks learn the
sound of each other's voices.

Emperor Penguin parents must find their chick among thousands after they return from fishing in the sea. The chicks call eagerly. In the deafening noise, the parent trumpets back until they are reunited.

If danger is near, a mother **Common Merganser** calls to her chicks, "Stay close." The family swims to safety.

A **Flamingo** chick peeps softly before it has even hatched. Its parent chirps back, offering encouragement to break free from the egg.

I'm not here.

Some birds use trickery
to protect themselves and
their nests.

The **American Bittern** has a loud booming call. But when danger draws near, she sits still as a stone. Her lie, "I'm not here," is convincing even to the keenest eye.

A **Sun Bittern** blends into her surroundings with striped brown and gray feathers. But if a hawk comes close, she fans her tail and flashes red patches on golden wings. "Stay back. I'm a devil-eyed monster!"

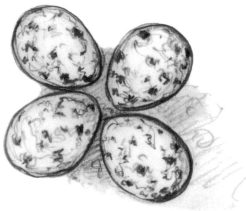

When a fox stalks near the nest of a **North American Killdeer**, Mama screams and flaps a wing awkwardly. Her broken-wing trick says, "Follow me, I'm injured, I'm a better meal." She stays just out of reach, luring the fox away from her eggs.

Look out! We're under attack!

Within a flock, birds communicate to protect themselves.

Caw, caw! An **American Crow** shrieks an alarm when a Great Horned Owl comes near. Instead of flying to safety, the flock joins her. They scold and mob the predator, chasing it away.

But when a crow prowls for eggs, **Scandinavian Fieldfares** declare war. *Chat, chat!* they warn. If the intruder doesn't flee, they dive at the crow dumping missiles of poop.

Sometimes it's safer to sound the alarm quietly. When a **Purple Finch** spots a hawk overhead, he makes a short *seet* call that says, "Keep quiet, danger is near." Quickly the flock takes cover.

A mother's call encourages her young.

A young **Peregrine Falcon** is nervous to take his first flight from high on a cliff nest. Mother sits in a nearby tree calling sharply with food. Eventually he flaps toward her. She continues the training until he can grab prey in mid-air.

A **Blue Jay** listens for the call of his hungry youngster. The fledgling has left the nest, but isn't ready to fly. Her parent answers with tender feeding calls as he brings her next meal.

Kuk, kuk, kuk. A Mother **Wood Duck** summons her chicks just after they've hatched. They can't fly, but they can swim and find food once they leave their tree nest.

Jump!

Listen and learn.

Some birds don't just sing from instinct alone, they learn to mimic, or imitate, the calls and songs of birds around them.

Baby **Scarlet Macaws** learn to mimic calls the way human babies learn to talk, by listening to their parents.

Northern Mockingbirds even mimic other bird songs. What better way to say to a mate, "Choose me, I'm the smartest." They can be noisy neighbors, even imitating man-made sounds like car alarms, ambulance sirens, and cell phone rings.

African Grey Parrots are excellent mimics. Many learn to repeat people's voices, but one named Alex learned to use words with human meaning. With his vocabulary of about 150 words, he could name objects, count to six, ask and answer questions, and request rewards. "Wanna nut!"

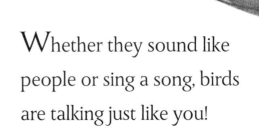

Whether they sound like people or sing a song, birds are talking just like you!

Birds in this book

 The **Blue Bird of Paradise** is one of the most brilliantly colored birds in the world. During courtship, it's the female who chooses her mate by tapping a male with her beak.
Habitat: mountain forests
Range: New Guinea

 The **American Goldfinch** is a popular bird at backyard feeders. It is the state bird of New Jersey, Iowa, and Washington. After breeding season, the male molts his bright yellow feathers and becomes a drabber color like the female.
Habitat: common in suburbs and fields and orchards
Range: across the United States and southern Canada

 American Robins are popular for their melodious songs and for bounding across lawns, tugging earthworms out of the ground. In fall and winter, they form large flocks and gather in trees to roost.
Habitat: common to parks, fields, and deciduous woodlands
Range: across North America

 Sage Grouse eat leaves, buds, stems, fruit, and insects. Only one or two males get picked by females each spring to mate. Then the females go off to nest and raise their chicks alone.
Habitat: sagebrush desert
Range: western United States

 Male **Wild Turkeys** don't help in raising young. After hatching, the chicks leave the nest almost immediately. They follow their mother and learn quickly to feed themselves on seeds, insects, buds, and small amphibians.
Habitat: forests with scattered openings
Range: throughout much of North America

 The **Palm Cockatoo** eats hard nuts and seeds with its powerful bill. Besides defending his territory, the male's drumming may also help a female find a hollow tree to make a nest cavity. Once bonded, a pair mates for life.
Habitat: rainforests and woodlands
Range: New Guinea and northern Australia

 The **Blue-Footed Booby** gets its name from its comical dance and clumsy walk. But they are agile flyers and spend their entire lives out at sea, only coming to shore to nest. They feed entirely on fish.
Habitat: the open sea
Range: nest on tropical and subtropical islands, and along the coastline of the Pacific Ocean

Western Grebe pairs present fish to one another before performing their courtship dance. Once mated, they build a floating nest, then work together to raise three or four chicks.
Habitat: lakes, marshes, and saltwater bays
Range: western United States and Canada

The **Indian Sarus Crane** is the tallest of all flying birds, standing 6 feet and with a wingspread of 8 feet. Though cranes are revered by many cultures, their populations have fallen drastically due to loss of habitat.
Habitat: wetlands, farmlands, and rice paddies
Range: northern India and western Nepal

European White Stork pairs breed for life and return to the same nest year after year. Many nest on man-made structures such as rooftops, towers, chimneys, and haystacks. Some nests have been in use for hundreds of years.
Habitat: wet pastures, flooded meadows, and shallow lakes
Range: throughout much of Europe, the Middle East, and parts of Asia and Africa.

Rhinoceros Hornbill males use chewed bark, food, and poop to seal the female inside the nest cavity so predators can't reach the eggs or young. When the chicks are ready to fly, the female chips away the wall to release herself and her young.
Habitat: rainforest
Range: Southeast Asia

Northern Gannets plunge from the air, diving as deep as 70 feet into the sea to catch fish. They breed in large colonies, with their nests just far enough apart so that neighbors' bills can't touch.
Habitat: the open sea
Range: nest on offshore islands and cliffs of the North Atlantic

The **Emperor Penguin** breeds in one of the coldest places on Earth. Unlike most birds, the father incubates the single egg, resting it on his feet and covering it with a flap of skin to keep it warm. After four months, his chick hatches.
Habitat: the open sea
Range: breeds on the stable ice pack of Antarctica

Common Merganser chicks leave the nest almost immediately, swimming alongside their mother and often hitching a ride on her back. These ducks have long bills with toothy projections to grip slippery fish they catch while diving.
Habitat: large lakes and rivers
Range: across most of North America

Flamingos nest in colonies. Male and female pairs work together to guard their single egg. A Flamingo's pink color comes from the food it eats, including algae, small aquatic insects, and crustaceans.
Habitat: large, shallow lakes or lagoons
Range: throughout much of Africa, Asia, North America, Central America, South America, and Europe

The **American Bittern** is an elusive kind of heron. From the shoreline, they wait motionless for long periods, then strike with their long bills to capture passing insects, fish, and amphibians.
Habitat: freshwater wetlands
Range: across the mid–United States to northern Canada

The **Sun Bittern** lives on the ground and rarely flies. It hunts fish, insects, and small animals. They are very quiet birds, communicating instead with their threatening display of spread wings and tail.
Habitat: wooded streams or creeks
Range: Central and South American rainforest

The **North American Killdeer** can be easily spotted running along the ground with its bold markings and high-pitched *kill-deer* call. They are often seen on gravel road shoulders where they nest.
Habitat: mudflats, meadows, road shoulders, and golf courses
Range: throughout North America

American Crows are intelligent, social birds that live in flocks. They usually feed on the ground and eat almost anything, from worms and insects, to small animals, fruit, seeds, and carrion (meat they find but don't kill themselves).
Habitat: common to fields, open woodlands, and forests
Range: throughout much of North America

A **Great Horned Owl** has a familiar deep *hoo-h'HOO-hoo-hoo* call. They prey on other birds and mammals, eating anything they can catch, even skunks! Like most owls, they hunt mostly at night.
Habitat: deserts, tundra, forests, and even suburban backyards
Range: widespread throughout North America

A **Scandinavian Fieldfare** is a large thrush. Adult males and females look similar, except that the female is a duller brown. They feed on worms, snails, insects, and fruit, and nest in colonies.
Habitat: fields, open country, and hedgerows
Range: breed throughout much of Europe

Purple Finches have a loud warbling song, but can be hard to see because they spend much of their time high in the trees. The best time to see them is in winter, when they eat seeds at backyard feeders.
Habitat: conifer forests
Range: breed in Canada and winter on the West Coast and eastern half of the United States.

The **Peregrine Falcon** is a raptor, a bird that hunts for food. They are the fastest of all birds, flying at speeds of 40 to 65 miles per hour, but can reach up to 200 mph when they dive to catch prey in mid-air. They sometimes nest on the side of city buildings.
Habitat: open areas that provide cliffs for nesting
Range: year round in western North America, winter along the East Coast and South America

The **Blue Jay** is a songbird familiar to many people for its pointy crest and noisy calls. Blue Jays are intelligent and have tight family bonds. Their favorite food is acorns. They have been known to mimic cat meows and sometimes a human voice.
Habitat: forest edges
Range: throughout the eastern half of the United States

The **Wood Duck** is one of the few ducks to nest in trees, using abandoned woodpecker holes and other cavities. They will also use man-made nest boxes if they are placed on trees near or above water. The male (drake) is one of the most colorful of all ducks.
Habitat: forested wetlands
Range: throughout most of North America

Scarlet Macaws are one of 17 species of macaws. These parrots have become scarce in the wild because of loss of habitat and because they are captured for the pet trade. Their heavy beaks are perfect for eating hard seeds and nuts, but they also eat fruits and insects.
Habitat: rainforests
Range: southern Mexico, through Central America to southern Brazil

Northern Mockingbirds are such good mimics that they fool even the best listener. If you hear a string of a dozen different birds singing outside your window, look and see—it may be only one mockingbird.
Habitat: towns, suburbs, backyards, parks, forest edges, and open land
Range: throughout the United States

African Grey Parrots are popular pets for their ability to mimic speech. But their numbers are declining in the wild because they are taken for the pet trade. Dr. Irene Pepperberg's research with Alex has led many to believe they are as intelligent as dolphins, chimpanzees, and human toddlers.
Habitat: rainforests
Range: West and Central Africa

Glossary

breed   To produce (give birth to or hatch) an offspring.

fledgling   A young bird that has left the nest and grown its flight feathers, but which may still need parental care.

flock   A number of birds of one kind that keep or feed together.

habitat   The place that is the natural environment for the life and growth of an animal or plant.

incubate   To sit upon eggs and keep them warm for the purpose of hatching.

instinct   A natural or inborn ability or pattern of behavior common to a given species.

mimic   To imitate or copy the song, sound, or behavior of another.

mob   To crowd around in large numbers in order to attack or annoy.

molt   To shed feathers that will be replaced by a new growth of feathers.

predator   A carnivorous animal that hunts, kills, and eats other animals in order to survive.

prey   An animal hunted or seized for food.

range   The region over which a population or species is distributed.

roost   To sit or rest on a perch, especially for the night.

species   A basic category of animals where all members resemble each other in appearance and are able to breed with other members.

territory   The area of land that an animal defends against intruders, especially from the same species.

References

Attenborough, David. *The Life of Birds.* London: BBC Books. 1998.

Friend, Tim. *Animal Talk: Breaking the Codes of Animal Language.* New York: Free Press. 2004.

Pepperberg, Irene. *Alex and Me: How a Scientist and a Parrot Uncovered a Hidden World of Animal Intelligence— and Formed a Deep Bond in the Process.* New York: HarperCollins. 2008.

Rothenberg, David. *Why Birds Sing: A Journey into the Mystery of Bird Song.* New York: Basic Books. 2005.

Web sites

Cornell Lab of Ornithology: http://www.birds.cornell.edu/

Author's note

I've always been fascinated by bird talk. Even as a little girl, I liked to walk in the woods and hoot until an owl hooted back. As I watched birds, I asked myself, *What do their calls and songs mean?* When scientists watch birds, they ask the same question. They observe bird behavior to find the meaning to their calls, songs, and other forms of interaction.

My grandparents were ornithologists, scientists who studied birds. My grandmother worked for years to breed Golden Eagles when the species was threatened. She observed her eagle so carefully, she could practically talk to it. Each spring the eagle called sharply, and my grandmother responded by bringing sticks. Then together they built a nest. Our family raised a variety of orphaned or injured birds as well. Some stayed for a lifetime; others grew strong and were released back to the wild.

I recorded songbirds in the mornings before school so I could learn to identify them by their calls. And I raised orphaned starlings who learned to mimic the call of my parakeet. At night, I lay in bed and listened to the screeching of barn owlets from their favorite roosting perch, the top of my grandmother's refrigerator. In the spring before dawn, we hiked in the desert and listened to Sage Grouse boom. Their ritual performance made me laugh—I thought their puffed up chests and inflated air sacs looked like hard-boiled eggs. But my favorite memory was canoeing alongside Western Grebes as they danced on water.

There is a fascinating variety to how birds call, sing, dance, strut, and boom. Watch the birds around you. Listen to the songs of goldfinches and robins until you can identify them by their call. Then watch their behavior to learn what their calls mean. If you become a good listener and keen observer, you can discover for yourself how birds communicate.

For Hammy

Thank you, Dave and Deirdre

Text and Illustrations copyright © 2012 by Lita Judge
Published by Flash Point, an imprint of Roaring Brook Press
Roaring Brook Press is a division of Holtzbrinck Publishing Holdings Limited Partnership
175 Fifth Avenue, New York, New York 10010
mackids.com

Library of Congress Cataloging-in-Publication Data
Judge, Lita.
    Bird Talk: what birds are saying and why / Lita Judge.— 1st ed.
        p.   cm.
    ISBN 978-1-59643-646-6
    1. Birds—Behavior—Juvenile literature.   2. Animal
communication—Juvenile literature.   3. Birdsongs—Juvenile literature.   I.
Title.
    QL698.3J83 2011
    598.159'4—dc22

                                                        2010030353

Roaring Brook Press books are available for special promotions and premiums.
    For details contact: Director of Special Markets, Holtzbrinck Publishers.

First edition 2012
Book design by Roberta Pressel
Printed in China by RR Donnelley Asia Printing Solutions. Ltd.,
Dongguan City, Guangdong Province

5   7   9   10   8   6   4